T0166904

SPIRIT
of
FAITH

the
ONENESS
of GOD

SPIRIT
of
FAITH

the
ONENESS
of GOD

compiled by Bahá'í Publishing

Bahá'í
PUBLISHING

Wilmette, Illinois

Bahá'í Publishing
415 Linden Avenue, Wilmette, Illinois 60091-2844
Copyright © 2010 by the National Spiritual Assembly of the
Bahá'ís of the United States

13   12   11   10   4   3   2   1

Library of Congress Cataloging-in-Publication Data

The oneness of God / compiled by Baha'i Publishing.
        p. cm. — (Spirit of faith series)
    Includes bibliographical references (p.   ).
    ISBN 978-1-931847-76-6 (alk. paper)
    1. God—Simplicity 2. Bahai Faith—Doctrines. I.
Bahá'u'lláh, 1817–1892. II. Bab, 'Ali Muhammad Shirazi,
1819–1850. III. 'Abdu'l-Bahá, 1844–1921. IV. Bahá'í Publishing Trust.
    BP370.O54 2010
    297.9'32112—dc22

                                                    2010021509

Cover design by Andrew Johnson
Book design by Patrick Falso

CONTENTS

INTRODUCTION

The Oneness of God is the first compilation in Bahá'í Publishing's *Spirit of Faith* series, which will explore weighty spiritual topics—such as the unity of humanity, the eternal covenant of God, the promise of world peace, and much more—by taking an in-depth look at how the writings of the Bahá'í Faith view these issues. Bahá'í Publishing hopes that this series will help bring the fundamental beliefs of the Bahá'í Faith to the receptive reader.

Bahá'ís believe in the essential unity of God, and the passages in this first compilation reveal that members of all religions are united in their devotion to the same one God, Who has progressively revealed teachings to humanity over time. We may have different names or traditions to praise Him, but ultimately God is one, and we are all part of His creation. The differences and conflicts in our world today are not the result of God's teachings; rather, they are the product of a humanity that has strayed far from its Creator and is in need of spiritual renewal. Included in this compilation are passages from the writings of Bahá'u'lláh, the Prophet and Founder of the Bahá'í Faith, Whose name means "the Glory of God"; those of His forerunner, the Báb; and the writings and recorded utterances of Bahá'u'lláh's eldest son and successor, 'Abdu'l-Bahá.

The Bahá'í Faith is an independent world religion that began in 1844 in Persia (present-day Iran). Since its inception, the Bahá'í Faith has spread to 235 nations and territories and has been accepted by more than five million people. Bahá'ís believe that there is only one God, that all the major world religions come from God, and that all the members of the human race are essentially members of one family. Bahá'ís strive to eliminate all forms of prejudice and believe that people of all races, nations, social statuses, and religious backgrounds are equal in the sight of God. The Bahá'í Faith also teaches that each individual is responsible for the independent investigation of truth, that science and religion are in harmony, and that men and women are equal in the sight of God.

It is hoped that these passages on the oneness of God will offer hope for a better future—one filled with unity, understanding, and acceptance between all peoples and religions of the world.

FROM THE
WRITINGS
OF
BAHÁ'U'LLÁH

1

O God, my God! I bear witness to Thy unity and Thy oneness, and that Thou art God, and that there is none other God but Thee. Thou hast everlastingly been sanctified above the mention of any one but Thee and the praise of all else except Thyself, and Thou wilt everlastingly continue to be the same as Thou wast from the beginning and hast ever been.

2

He is a true believer in Divine unity who, far from confusing duality with oneness, refuseth to allow any notion of multiplicity to becloud his conception of the singleness of God, who will regard the Divine Being as One Who, by His very nature, transcendeth the limitations of numbers.

3

I beg of Thee, O my God, by Thy power, and Thy might, and Thy sovereignty, which have embraced all who are in Thy heaven and on Thy earth, to make known unto Thy servants this luminous Way and this straight Path, that they may acknowledge Thy unity and Thy oneness, with a certainty which the vain imaginations of the doubters will not impair, nor the idle fancies of the wayward obscure. Illumine, O my Lord, the eyes of Thy servants, and brighten their hearts with the splendors of the light of Thy knowledge, that they may apprehend the greatness of this most sublime station, and recognize this most luminous Horizon: . . .

4

B ear thou witness in thine inmost heart unto this testimony which God hath Himself and for Himself pronounced, that there is none other God but Him, that all else besides Him have been created by His behest, have been fashioned by His leave, are subject to His law, are as a thing forgotten when compared to the glorious evidences of His oneness, and are as nothing when brought face to face with the mighty revelations of His unity.

5

Who is there, O my God, that can be deemed worthy to be remembered when Thou art remembered, and where is he to be found who can be regarded as capable of hinting at Thy nature or worthy of mention in the court of Thy transcendent oneness? From everlasting Thou hast been alone with no one else beside Thee, and to everlasting Thou wilt continue to be one and the same. No God is there beside Thee, the God of power, of glory and wisdom.

6

The essence of belief in Divine unity consisteth in regarding Him Who is the Manifestation of God and Him Who is the invisible, the inaccessible, the unknowable Essence as one and the same. By this is meant that whatever pertaineth to the former, all His acts and doings, whatever He ordaineth or forbiddeth, should be considered, in all their aspects, and under all circumstances, and without any reservation, as identical with the Will of God Himself. This is the loftiest station to which a true believer in the unity of God can ever hope to attain. Blessed is the man that reacheth this station, and is of them that are steadfast in their belief.

7

Beware, O believers in the Unity of God, lest ye be tempted to make any distinction between any of the Manifestations of His Cause, or to discriminate against the signs that have accompanied and proclaimed their Revelation. This indeed is the true meaning of Divine Unity, if ye be of them that apprehend and believe this truth. Be ye assured, moreover, that the works and acts of each and every one of these Manifestations of God, nay whatever pertaineth unto them, and whatsoever they may manifest in the future, are all ordained by God, and are a reflection of His Will and Purpose. Whoso maketh the slightest possible difference between their persons, their words, their messages, their acts and manners, hath indeed disbelieved in God, hath repudiated His signs, and betrayed the Cause of His Messengers.

8

We testify, O my God, that Thou art God, and that there is no God besides Thee. From eternity Thou hast existed with none to equal or rival Thee, and wilt abide for ever the same. I beseech Thee, by the eyes which see Thee stablished upon the throne of unity and the seat of oneness, to aid all them that love Thee by Thy Most Great Name, and to lift them up into such heights that they will testify with their own beings and with their tongues that Thou art God alone, the Incomparable, the One, the Ever-Abiding. Thou hast had at no time any peer or partner. Thou, in truth, art the All-Glorious, the Almighty, Whose help is implored by all men.

9

I testify, O my God, that Thou hast, from eternity, sent down upon Thy servants naught else except that which can cause them to soar up and be drawn near unto Thee, and to ascend into the heaven of Thy transcendent oneness.

10

He is really a believer in the Unity of God who recognizeth in each and every created thing the sign of the revelation of Him Who is the Eternal Truth, and not he who maintaineth that the creature is indistinguishable from the Creator.

11

A twofold obligation resteth upon him who hath recognized the Dayspring of the Unity of God, and acknowledged the truth of Him Who is the Manifestation of His oneness. The first is steadfastness in His love, such steadfastness that neither the clamor of the enemy nor the claims of the idle pretender can deter him from cleaving unto Him Who is the Eternal Truth, a steadfastness that taketh no account of them whatever. The second is strict observance of the laws He hath prescribed—laws which He hath always ordained, and will continue to ordain, unto men, and through which the truth may be distinguished and separated from falsehood.

12

He is indeed a true believer in the unity of God who, in this Day, will regard Him as One immeasurably exalted above all the comparisons and likenesses with which men have compared Him. He hath erred grievously who hath mistaken these comparisons and likenesses for God Himself. Consider the relation between the craftsman and his handiwork, between the painter and his painting. Can it ever be maintained that the work their hands have produced is the same as themselves? By Him Who is the Lord of the Throne above and of earth below! They can be regarded in no other light except as evidences that proclaim the excellence and perfection of their author.

13

I am he, O my God, who testifieth to Thy unity, who acknowledgeth Thy oneness, who boweth humbly before the revelations of Thy majesty, and who recognizeth with downcast countenance the splendors of the light of Thy transcendent glory.

14

All praise to the unity of God, and all honor to Him, the sovereign Lord, the incomparable and all-glorious Ruler of the universe, Who, out of utter nothingness, hath created the reality of all things, Who, from naught, hath brought into being the most refined and subtle elements of His creation, and Who, rescuing His creatures from the abasement of remoteness and the perils of ultimate extinction, hath received them into His kingdom of incorruptible glory. Nothing short of His all-encompassing grace, His all-pervading mercy, could have possibly achieved it. How could it, otherwise, have been possible for sheer nothingness to have acquired by itself the worthiness and capacity to emerge from its state of non-existence into the realm of being?

15

The Pen of the Most High hath, at all times and under all conditions, remembered, with joy and tenderness, His loved ones, and hath counseled them to follow in His way. Well is it with him whom the changes and chances of this world have failed to deter from recognizing the Dayspring of the Unity of God, who hath quaffed, with unswerving resolve, and in the name of the Self-Subsisting, the sealed wine of His Revelation. Such a man shall be numbered with the inmates of Paradise, in the Book of God, the Lord of all worlds.

16

Witness how the divers peoples and kindreds of the earth bear witness to His unity, and recognize His oneness. But for the sign of the Unity of God within them, they would have never acknowledged the truth of the words, "There is none other God but God."

17

Whither shall I turn, O my God, powerless as I am to discover any other way except the way Thou didst set before Thy chosen Ones? All the atoms of the earth proclaim Thee to be God, and testify that there is none other God besides Thee. Thou hast from eternity been powerful to do what Thou hast willed, and to ordain what Thou hast pleased.

18

All created things have borne witness unto that which the Tongue of Thy grandeur hath testified ere their creation. Verily Thou art God; there is none other God but Thee! From everlasting Thou wast sanctified from the mention of Thy servants, and exalted above the description of Thy creatures.

19

Enable, then, Thy servants, O my God, to recognize the Day-Star that hath shone forth above the horizon of Thine irrevocable decree and purpose, and suffer them not to be deprived of the Paradise which Thou, by Thy name, the All-Glorious, hast called into being in the heavens of Thine exalted omnipotence. Cause them, moreover, O my God, to hearken to Thy most sweet voice, that they may all hasten to recognize Thy unity and acknowledge Thy oneness, O Thou Who art the Beloved of the hearts of all that yearn after Thee, and the Object of the adoration of such as have known Thee!

20

Assist Thou Thy servants, O my Lord, to recognize Thy unity and to declare Thy oneness, that all may gather together around what Thou didst desire in this Day whereon the sun of Thine essence hath shone forth above the horizon of Thy will, and the moon of Thine own being hath risen from the Day-Spring of Thy behest. Thou art He, O my Lord, from Whose knowledge nothing whatsoever escapeth, and Whom no one can frustrate. Thou doest Thy pleasure, by Thy sovereignty that overshadoweth the worlds.

21

The light that is shed from the heaven of bounty, and the benediction that shineth from the dawning-place of the will of God, the Lord of the Kingdom of Names, rest upon Him Who is the Supreme Mediator, the Most Exalted Pen, Him Whom God hath made the Dawning-Place of His most excellent names and the Dayspring of His most exalted attributes. Through Him the light of unity hath shone forth above the horizon of the world, and the law of oneness hath been revealed amidst the nations, who, with radiant faces, have turned towards the Supreme Horizon, and acknowledged that which the Tongue of Utterance hath spoken in the kingdom of His knowledge:

"Earth and heaven, glory and dominion, are God's, the Omnipotent, the Almighty, the Lord of grace abounding!"

22

Whatsoever in the contingent world can either be expressed or apprehended, can never transgress the limits which, by its inherent nature, have been imposed upon it. God, alone, transcendeth such limitations. He, verily, is from everlasting. No peer or partner has been, or can ever be, joined with Him. No name can be compared with His Name. No pen can portray His nature, neither can any tongue depict His glory. He will, forever, remain immeasurably exalted above any one except Himself.

23

Tear asunder, in My Name, the veils that have grievously blinded your vision, and, through the power born of your belief in the unity of God, scatter the idols of vain imitation. Enter, then, the holy paradise of the good-pleasure of the All-Merciful. Sanctify your souls from whatsoever is not of God, and taste ye the sweetness of rest within the pale of His vast and mighty Revelation, and beneath the shadow of His supreme and infallible authority.

24

We have accepted to be abased, O believers in the Unity of God, that ye may be exalted, and have suffered manifold afflictions, that ye might prosper and flourish.

25

This Wronged One exhorteth thee as He hath exhorted thee before, and hath never had any wish for thee save that thou shouldst enter the ocean of the unity of God, the Lord of the worlds. This is the day whereon all created things cry out, and announce unto men this Revelation, through which hath appeared what was concealed and preserved in the knowledge of God, the Mighty, the All-Praised.

26

Behold me, then, O my God, fallen prostrate upon the dust before Thee, confessing my powerlessness and Thine omnipotence, my poverty and Thy wealth, mine evanescence and Thine eternity, mine utter abasement and Thine infinite glory. I recognize that there is none other God but Thee, that Thou hast no peer nor partner, none to equal or rival Thee. In Thine unapproachable loftiness Thou hast, from eternity, been exalted above the praise of any one but Thee, and shalt continue for ever, in Thy transcendent singleness and glory, to be sanctified from the glorification of any one except Thine own Self.

27

Glorified art Thou, O Lord my God! My tongue, both the tongue of my body and the tongue of my heart, my limbs and members, every pulsating vein within me, every hair of my head, all proclaim that Thou art God, and that there is none other God beside Thee. From everlasting Thou hast been immeasurably exalted above all similitudes and comparisons, and sanctified from whatsoever pertaineth to the creation Thou hast created and fashioned. From eternity Thou hast been alone, with none to share the majesty of Thy singleness, and hast remained far above the changes and chances to which all Thy creatures are subjected.

28

I bear witness to Thy unity and Thy oneness, and that Thou art God, and that there is none other God beside Thee. Thou hast, verily, revealed Thy Cause, fulfilled Thy Covenant, and opened wide the door of Thy grace to all that dwell in heaven and on earth. Blessing and peace, salutation and glory, rest upon Thy loved ones, whom the changes and chances of the world have not deterred from turning unto Thee, and who have given their all, in the hope of obtaining that which is with Thee. Thou art, in truth, the Ever-Forgiving, the All-Bountiful.

29

Whoso accepteth and recognizeth that which is written down at this moment by the Pen of Glory is indeed reckoned in the Book of God, the Lord of the beginning and the end, among the exponents of divine unity, they that uphold the concept of the oneness of God.

30

Thy unity is inscrutable, O my God, to all except them that have recognized Him Who is the Manifestation of Thy singleness and the Day-Spring of Thy oneness.

31

They that have truly recognized the Unity of God should be regarded as the primary manifestations of this Name. It is they who have quaffed the wine of Divine Unity from the cup which the hand of God hath proffered unto them, and who have turned their faces towards Him. How vast the distance that separateth these sanctified beings from those men that are so far away from God!

32

It is evident to thee that the Bearers of the trust of God are made manifest unto the peoples of the earth as the Exponents of a new Cause and the Bearers of a new Message. Inasmuch as these Birds of the Celestial Throne are all sent down from the heaven of the Will of God, and as they all arise to proclaim His irresistible Faith, they therefore are regarded as one soul and the same person. For they all drink from the one Cup of the love of God, and all partake of the fruit of the same Tree of Oneness.

33

Defer ye humbly to the faithful, they that have believed in God and in His signs, whose hearts witness to His unity, whose tongues proclaim His oneness, and who speak not except by His leave.

34

The purpose of God in creating man hath been, and will ever be, to enable him to know his Creator and to attain His Presence. To this most excellent aim, this supreme objective, all the heavenly Books and the divinely-revealed and weighty Scriptures unequivocally bear witness.

35

Magnified be Thy name, O Lord my God! Thou art He Whom all things worship and Who worshipeth no one, Who is the Lord of all things and is the vassal of none, Who knoweth all things and is known of none. Thou didst wish to make Thyself known unto men; therefore, Thou didst, through a word of Thy mouth, bring creation into being and fashion the universe. There is none other God except Thee, the Fashioner, the Creator, the Almighty, the Most Powerful.

36

How wondrous is the unity of the Living, the Ever-Abiding God—a unity which is exalted above all limitations, that transcendeth the comprehension of all created things! He hath, from everlasting, dwelt in His inaccessible habitation of holiness and glory, and will unto everlasting continue to be enthroned upon the heights of His independent sovereignty and grandeur. How lofty hath been His incorruptible Essence, how completely independent of the knowledge of all created things, and how immensely exalted will it remain above the praise of all the inhabitants of the heavens and the earth!

37

It behooveth thee and those like thee to submit yourselves to them Who are the Manifestations of the unity of God, and to defer humbly to the faithful, who have forsaken their all for the sake of God, and have detached themselves from the things which engross men's attention, and lead them astray from the path of God, the All-Glorious, the All-Praised. Thus do We send down upon you that which shall profit you and profit them that have placed their whole trust and confidence in their Lord.

38

I know not, O my God, how long will Thy creatures continue to slumber on the bed of forgetfulness and evil desires, and remain far removed from Thee and shut out from Thy presence. Draw them nearer, O my God, unto the scene of Thine effulgent glory, and enrapture their hearts with the sweet savors of Thine inspiration, through which they who adore Thy unity have soared on the wings of desire towards Thee, and they who are devoted to Thee have reached unto Him Who is the Dawning-Place of the Day-Star of Thy creation.

39

I entreat Thee, therefore, O my God, by Thy Name through which Thou hast guided Thy lovers to the living waters of Thy grace and Thy favors, and attracted them that long for Thee to the Paradise of Thy nearness and Thy presence, to open the eyes of Thy people that they may recognize in this Revelation the manifestation of Thy transcendent unity, and the dawning of the lights of Thy countenance and Thy beauty.

40

I implore Thee, O my God and my Master, by Thy word through which they who have believed in Thy unity have soared up into the atmosphere of Thy knowledge, and they who are devoted to Thee have ascended into the heaven of Thy oneness, to inspire Thy loved ones with that which will assure their hearts in Thy Cause. Endue them with such steadfastness that nothing whatsoever will hinder them from turning towards Thee.

41

Thou beholdest, O my God, how every bone in my body soundeth like a pipe with the music of Thine inspiration, revealing the signs of Thy oneness and the clear tokens of Thy unity. I entreat Thee, O my God, by Thy Name which irradiateth all things, to raise up such servants as shall incline their ears to the voice of the melodies that hath ascended from the right hand of the throne of Thy glory. Make them, then, to quaff from the hand of Thy grace the wine of Thy mercy, that it may assure their hearts, and cause them to turn away from the left hand of idle fancies and vain imaginings to the right hand of confidence and certitude.

42

O people of God! In this day everyone should fix his eyes upon the horizon of these blessed words: "Alone and unaided He doeth whatsoever He pleaseth." Whoso attaineth this station hath verily attained the light of the essential unity of God and is enlightened thereby. . . .

43

God grant that, with a penetrating vision, thou mayest perceive, in all things, the sign of the revelation of Him Who is the Ancient King, and recognize how exalted and sanctified from the whole creation is that most holy and sacred Being. This, in truth, is the very root and essence of belief in the unity and singleness of God. "God was alone; there was none else besides Him." He, now, is what He hath ever been. There is none other God but Him, the One, the Incomparable, the Almighty, the Most Exalted, the Most Great.

44

God testifieth to the unity of His Godhood and to the singleness of His own Being. On the throne of eternity, from the inaccessible heights of His station, His tongue proclaimeth that there is none other God but Him. He Himself, independently of all else, hath ever been a witness unto His own oneness, the revealer of His own nature, the glorifier of His own essence. He, verily, is the All-Powerful, the Almighty, the Beauteous.

45

The Bearers of the Trust of God are made manifest unto the peoples of the earth as the Exponents of a new Cause and the Revealers of a new Message. Inasmuch as these Birds of the celestial Throne are all sent down from the heaven of the Will of God, and as they all arise to proclaim His irresistible Faith, they, therefore, are regarded as one soul and the same person. For they all drink from the one Cup of the love of God, and all partake of the fruit of the same Tree of Oneness.

46

I am the one, O Lord, whose heart and soul, whose limbs, whose inner and outer tongue testify to Thy unity and Thy oneness, and bear witness that Thou art God and that there is no God but Thee.

47

Since Thou hast purposed, O my God, to cause all created things to enter into the tabernacle of Thy transcendent grace and favor, and to waft over the entire creation the fragrances of the raiment of Thy glorious unity, and to look upon all things with the eyes of Thy bounty and Thy oneness, I beseech Thee, therefore, by Thy love, which Thou hast made to be the mainspring of the revelations of Thine eternal holiness, and the flame that gloweth within the hearts of such of Thy creatures as yearn towards Thee, to create, this very moment, for those of Thy people who are wholly devoted to Thee, and for such of Thy loved ones as love Thee, out of the essence of Thy bounty and Thy generosity, and from the inmost spirit of Thy grace and Thy glory, Thy Paradise of transcendent holiness, and to exalt it above everything except Thee, and to sanctify it from aught else save Thyself.

48

Cause us, then, to be so steadfast in our love towards Thee that we will turn to none except Thee, and will be reckoned amongst them that are brought nigh to Thee, and acknowledge Thee as One Who is exalted above every comparison and is holy beyond all likeness, and will lift up our voices amongst Thy servants and cry aloud that He is the one God, the Incomparable, the Ever-Abiding, the Most Powerful, the All-Glorious, the All-Wise.

49

Since Thou hast, O my God, established Thyself upon the throne of Thy transcendent unity, and ascended the mercy seat of Thy oneness, it befitteth Thee to blot out from the hearts of all beings whatsoever may keep them back from gaining admittance into the sanctuary of Thy Divine mysteries, and may shut them out from the tabernacle of Thy Divinity, that all hearts may mirror Thy beauty, and may reveal Thee, and speak of Thee, and that all created things may show forth the tokens of Thy most august sovereignty, and shed the splendors of the light of Thy most holy governance, and that all who are in heaven and on earth may laud and magnify Thy unity, and give Thee glory, for having manifested Thy Self unto them through Him Who is the Revealer of Thy oneness.

50

Praise be to God, the Ancient, the Ever-Abiding, the Changeless, the Eternal! He Who hath testified in His Own Being that verily He is the One, the Single, the Untrammelled, the Exalted. We bear witness that verily there is no God but Him, acknowledging His oneness, confessing His singleness. He hath ever dwelt in unapproachable heights, in the summits of His loftiness, sanctified from the mention of aught save Himself, free from the description of aught but Him.

51

There can be no doubt whatever that the peoples of the world, of whatever race or religion, derive their inspiration from one heavenly Source, and are the subjects of one God. The difference between the ordinances under which they abide should be attributed to the varying requirements and exigencies of the age in which they were revealed. All of them, except a few which are the outcome of human perversity, were ordained of God, and are a reflection of His Will and Purpose. Arise and, armed with the power of faith, shatter to pieces the gods of your vain imaginings, the sowers of dissension amongst you. Cleave unto that which draweth you together and uniteth you. This, verily, is the most exalted Word which the Mother Book hath sent down and revealed unto you. To this beareth witness the Tongue of Grandeur from His habitation of glory.

52

And as the human heart, as fashioned by God, is one and undivided, it behooveth thee to take heed that its affections be, also, one and undivided. Cleave thou, therefore, with the whole affection of thine heart, unto His love, and withdraw it from the love of any one besides Him, that He may aid thee to immerse thyself in the ocean of His unity, and enable thee to become a true upholder of His oneness.

53

Consider . . . the revelation of the light of the Name of God, the Incomparable. Behold, how this light hath enveloped the entire creation, how each and every thing manifesteth the sign of His Unity, testifieth to the reality of Him Who is the Eternal Truth, proclaimeth His sovereignty, His oneness, and His power.

54

I have set my face towards Thy Cause, believing in Thy oneness, acknowledging Thy unity, recognizing Thy sovereignty and the power of Thy might, and confessing the greatness of Thy majesty and glory.

55

From eternity Thou hast, in Thy transcendent oneness, been immeasurably exalted above Thy servants' conception of Thy unity, and wilt to eternity remain, in Thine unapproachable singleness, far above the praise of Thy creatures. No words that any one beside Thee may utter can ever beseem Thee, and no man's description except Thine own description can befit Thy nature. All who adore Thy unity have been sore perplexed to fathom the mystery of Thy oneness, and all have confessed their powerlessness to attain unto the comprehension of Thine essence and to scale the pinnacle of Thy knowledge.

56

O God, my God, and my Desire, and my Adored One, and my Master, and my Mainstay, and my utmost Hope, and my supreme Aspiration! Thou seest me turning towards Thee, holding fast unto the cord of Thy bounty, clinging to the hem of Thy generosity, acknowledging the sanctity of Thy Self and the purity of Thine Essence, and testifying to Thy unity and Thy oneness. I bear witness that Thou art the One, the Single, the Incomparable, the Ever-Abiding.

57

Unto Thee be praise, O Lord my God! I testify that Thou art God, and that there is none other God besides Thee. Thou hast from eternity been immeasurably exalted above the praise of any one except Thee, and far above the description of any of Thy creatures. All created things have borne witness to Thy unity, and every dweller in Thy kingdom hath confessed Thy oneness.

58

I have recognized Thy truth in Thy days, and have directed my steps towards the shores of Thy oneness, confessing Thy singleness, acknowledging Thy unity, and hoping for Thy forgiveness and pardon. Powerful art Thou to do what Thou willest; no God is there beside Thee, the All-Glorious, the Ever-Forgiving.

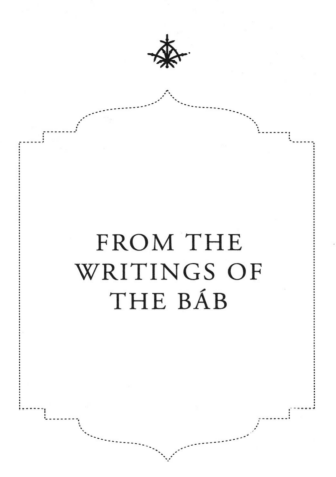

FROM THE WRITINGS OF THE BÁB

1

There is no paradise more wondrous for any soul than to be exposed to God's Manifestation in His Day, to hear His verses and believe in them, to attain His presence, which is naught but the presence of God, to sail upon the sea of the heavenly kingdom of His good-pleasure, and to partake of the choice fruits of the paradise of His divine Oneness.

2

Indeed God is but one God, and far be it from His glory that there should be aught else besides Him. All those who shall attain unto Him on the Day of Resurrection are but His servants, and God is, of a truth, a sufficient Protector. Verily I am none other but the servant of God and His Word, and none but the first one to bow down in supplication before God, the Most Exalted; and indeed God witnesseth all things.

3

The One true God may be compared unto the sun and the believer unto a mirror. No sooner is the mirror placed before the sun than it reflects its light.

4

God's existence in itself testifieth to His Own oneness, while every created thing, by its very nature, beareth evidence that it hath been fashioned by God.

5

Lauded and glorified art Thou, O Lord! Both the world of existence and the souls of men bear witness that Thou art transcendent above the revelations of Thy handiwork, and the bearers of Thy names and attributes proclaim that Thou art immeasurably exalted above such praise as the dwellers of the dominions of creation and invention may render unto Thee. All appearances and realities indicate the oneness of Thine Essence, and all evidences and signs reflect the truth that Thou art God and there is no peer or partner for Thee throughout the kingdoms of heaven and earth.

6

Say, God is the Lord and all are worshippers unto Him.

Say, God is the True One and all pay homage unto Him.

This is God, your Lord, and unto Him shall ye return.

Is there any doubt concerning God? He hath created you and all things. The Lord of all worlds is He.

7

A true believer in the unity of God who keepeth his eyes directed towards Him alone will regard aught else but Him as utter nothingness.

8

Throughout eternity Thou hast been, O my Lord, and wilt ever remain the One true God, while all else save Thee are needy and poor. Having clung tenaciously to Thy Cord, O my God, I have detached myself from all mankind, and having set my face towards the habitation of Thy tender mercy, I have turned away from all created things. Graciously inspire me, O my God, through Thy grace and bounty, Thy glory and majesty, and Thy dominion and grandeur, for no one mighty and all-knowing can I find beside Thee. Protect me, O my God, through the potency of Thy transcendent and all-sufficing glory and by the hosts of the heavens and the earth, inasmuch as in no one can I wholly place my trust but in Thee and no refuge is there but Thee.

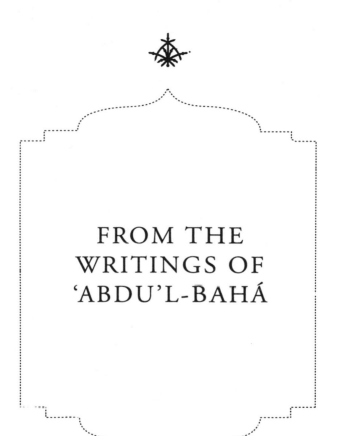

FROM THE
WRITINGS OF
'ABDU'L-BAHÁ

1

The divine religions must be the cause of one-ness among men, and the means of unity and love; they must promulgate universal peace, free man from every prejudice, bestow joy and gladness, exercise kindness to all men and do away with every difference and distinction.

2

How good it is if the friends be as close as sheaves of light, if they stand together side by side in a firm unbroken line. For now have the rays of reality from the Sun of the world of existence, united in adoration all the worshipers of this light; and these rays have, through infinite grace, gathered all peoples together within this wide-spreading shelter; therefore must all souls become as one soul, and all hearts as one heart. Let all be set free from the multiple identities that were born of passion and desire, and in the oneness of their love for God find a new way of life.

3

O thou believer in the oneness of God! Know thou that nothing profiteth a soul save the love of the All-Merciful, nothing lighteth up a heart save the splendor that shineth from the realm of the Lord.

Forsake thou every other concern, let oblivion overtake the memory of all else. Confine thy thoughts to whatever will lift up the human soul to the Paradise of heavenly grace, and make every bird of the Kingdom wing its way unto the Supreme Horizon, the central point of everlasting honor in this contingent world.

4

The unity which is productive of unlimited results is first a unity of mankind which recognizes that all are sheltered beneath the overshadowing glory of the All-Glorious, that all are servants of one God; for all breathe the same atmosphere, live upon the same earth, move beneath the same heavens, receive effulgence from the same sun and are under the protection of one God.

5

All the divine Manifestations have proclaimed the oneness of God and the unity of mankind. They have taught that men should love and mutually help each other in order that they might progress. Now if this conception of religion be true, its essential principle is the oneness of humanity. The fundamental truth of the Manifestations is peace. This underlies all religion, all justice. The divine purpose is that men should live in unity, concord and agreement and should love one another.

6

If you arise in the Cause of God with divine power, heavenly grace, the sincerity of the Kingdom, a merciful heart and decisive intention, it is certain that the world of humanity will be entirely illumined, the moralities of mankind will become merciful, the foundations of the Most Great Peace will be laid, and the oneness of the kingdom of man will become a reality.

7

Bahá'u'lláh teaches that the world of humanity is in need of the breath of the Holy Spirit, for in spiritual quickening and enlightenment true oneness is attained with God and man.

8

A man should pause and reflect and be just: his Lord, out of measureless grace, has made him a human being and honored him with the words: "Verily, We created man in the goodliest of forms"*—and caused His mercy which rises out of the dawn of oneness to shine down upon him, until he became the wellspring of the words of God and the place where the mysteries of heaven alighted, and on the morning of creation he was covered with the rays of the qualities of perfection and the graces of holiness.

---

* Qur'án 95:4.

9

We are striving with heart and soul, resting neither day nor night, seeking not a moment's ease, to make this world of man the mirror of the unity of God. Then how much more must the beloved of the Lord reflect that unity?

10

Now is the time for the lovers of God to raise high the banners of unity, to intone, in the assemblages of the world, the verses of friendship and love and to demonstrate to all that the grace of God is one.

11

The divine Manifestations since the day of Adam have striven to unite humanity so that all may be accounted as one soul. The function and purpose of a shepherd is to gather and not disperse his flock. The Prophets of God have been divine Shepherds of humanity. They have established a bond of love and unity among mankind, made scattered peoples one nation and wandering tribes a mighty kingdom. They have laid the foundation of the oneness of God and summoned all to universal peace. All these holy, divine Manifestations are one. They have served one God, promulgated the same truth, founded the same institutions and reflected the same light.

12

We must go back to the foundation upon which human solidarity rests—namely, that all are the progeny of Adam, the creatures and servants of one God; that God is the Protector and Provider; that all are submerged in the sea of divine mercy and grace and God is loving toward all.

13

Now must we . . . bind ourselves together in the utmost unity, be kind and loving to each other, sacrificing all our possessions, our honor, yea, even our lives for each other. Then will it be proved that we have acted according to the teachings of God, that we have been real believers in the oneness of God and unity of mankind.

14

The Ancient Beauty was ever, during His sojourn in this transitory world, either a captive bound with chains, or living under a sword, or subjected to extreme suffering and torment, or held in the Most Great Prison. Because of His physical weakness, brought on by His afflictions, His blessed body was worn away to a breath; it was light as a cobweb from long grieving. And His reason for shouldering this heavy load and enduring all this anguish, which was even as an ocean that hurleth its waves to high heaven—His reason for putting on the heavy iron chains and for becoming the very embodiment of utter resignation and meekness, was to lead every soul on earth to concord, to fellow feeling, to oneness; to make known amongst all peoples the sign of the singleness of God, so that at last the primal oneness deposited at the heart of all created things would bear its destined fruit, and the splendor of "No difference canst thou see in the creation of the God of Mercy,"* would cast abroad its rays.

* Qur'án 67:3.

15

Now is the time for the lovers of God to raise high the banners of unity, to intone, in the assemblages of the world, the verses of friendship and love and to demonstrate to all that the grace of God is one. Thus will the tabernacles of holiness be upraised on the summits of the earth, gathering all peoples into the protective shadow of the Word of Oneness. This great bounty will dawn over the world at the time when the lovers of God shall arise to carry out His Teachings, and to scatter far and wide the fresh, sweet scents of universal love.

16

So intensely hath the glory of Divine Unity penetrated souls and hearts that all are now bound one to another with heavenly ties, and all are even as a single heart, a single soul. Wherefore reflections of the spirit and impressions of the Divine are now mirrored clear and sharp in the deep heart's core. I beg of God to strengthen these spiritual bonds as day followeth day, and make this mystic oneness to shine ever more brightly, until at last all shall be as troops marshaled together beneath the banner of the Covenant within the sheltering shade of the Word of God; that they may strive with all their might until universal fellowship, close and warm, and unalloyed love, and spiritual relationships, will connect all the hearts in the world. Then will all humankind, because of this fresh and dazzling bounty, be gathered in a single homeland. Then will conflict and dissension vanish from the face of the earth, then will mankind be cradled in love for the beauty of the All-Glorious. Discord will change to accord, dissension to unison. The roots of malevolence will be torn out, the basis of aggression destroyed. The bright rays of union will obliterate the darkness of limitations, and the splendors of heaven will make the human heart to be even as a mine veined richly with the love of God.

17

At a time when warfare and strife prevailed among nations, when enmity and hatred separated sects and denominations and human differences were very great, Bahá'u'lláh appeared upon the horizon of the East, proclaiming the oneness of God and the unity of the world of humanity. He promulgated the teaching that all mankind are the servants of one God; that all have come into being through the bestowal of the one Creator; that God is kind to all, nurtures, rears and protects all, provides for all and extends His love and mercy to all races and people.

18

We . . . must strive in this pathway of love and service, sacrificing life and possessions, passing our days in devotion, consecrating our efforts wholly to the Cause of God so that, God willing, the ensign of universal religion may be uplifted in the world of mankind and the oneness of the world of humanity be established.

19

The Prophets of God voiced the spirit of unity and agreement. They have been the Founders of divine reality. Therefore, if the nations of the world forsake imitations and investigate the reality underlying the revealed Word of God, they will agree and become reconciled. For reality is one and not multiple.

20

God has destined and intended religion to be the cause and means of cooperative effort and accomplishment among mankind. To this end He has sent the Prophets of God, the holy Manifestations of the Word, in order that the fundamental reality and religion of God may prove to be the bond of human unity, for the divine religions revealed by these holy Messengers have one and the same foundation.

21

All human creatures are the servants of God. All are submerged in the sea of His mercy. The Creator of all is one God; the Provider, the Giver, the Protector of all is one God. He is kind to all; why should we be unkind? All live beneath the shadow of His love; why should we hate each other? There are certain people who are ignorant; they must be educated. Some are like children; they must be trained and educated until they reach maturity. Others are sickly, intellectually ill, spiritually ill; they must be treated and healed. But all are the servants of God.

22

Service in love for mankind is unity with God. He who serves has already entered the Kingdom and is seated at the right hand of his Lord.

23

The real temple is the very Word of God; for to it all humanity must turn, and it is the center of unity for all mankind.

24

It is daybreak, and from the rising-point of the invisible realms of God, the light of unity is dawning; and streaming and beating down from the hidden world of the Kingdom of oneness there cometh a flood of abounding grace. Glad tidings of the Kingdom are sounding from every side, and wafting in from every direction are the first morning signs of the exalting of God's Word and the upraising of His Cause.

25

Wherefore, O beloved of the Lord, strive ye with heart and soul to receive a share of His holy attributes and take your portion of the bounties of His sanctity—that ye may become the tokens of unity, the standards of singleness, and seek out the meaning of oneness; that ye may, in this garden of God, lift up your voices and sing the blissful anthems of the spirit. Become ye as the birds who offer Him their thanks, and in the blossoming bowers of life chant ye such melodies as will dazzle the minds of those who know. Raise ye a banner on the highest peaks of the world, a flag of God's favor to ripple and wave in the winds of His grace; plant ye a tree in the field of life, amid the roses of this visible world, that will yield a fruitage fresh and sweet.

26

There is perfect brotherhood underlying humanity, for all are servants of one God and belong to one family under the protection of divine providence.

27

B ahá'u'lláh appeared upon the divine horizon, even as the glory of the sun, and in that gross darkness and hopelessness of the human world there shone a great light. He founded the oneness of the world of humanity, declaring that all mankind are as sheep and that God is the real and true Shepherd. The Shepherd is one, and all people are of His flock.

28

May the world of humanity find peace and composure and this dark earth be transformed into a realm of radiance. May the East and West clasp hands together. May the oneness of God become reflected and fully revealed in the hearts of humanity and all mankind prove to be the manifestations of the favors of God.

29

He [Bahá'u'lláh] proclaimed the oneness of the world of humanity and announced that all are the servants of God. He taught that all the religions are beneath the shadow and protection of the Almighty, that God is compassionate and loving to all, that the revelations of all the Prophets of the past have been in perfect unity and agreement, that the heavenly Books have confirmed each other; therefore, why should contention and strife exist among the people?

30

We must be united. We must love each other. We must ever praise each other. We must bestow commendation upon all people, thus removing the discord and hatred which have caused alienation amongst men. Otherwise, the conditions of the past will continue, praising ourselves and condemning others; religious wars will have no end, and religious prejudice, the prime cause of this havoc and tribulation, will increase. This must be abandoned, and the way to do it is to investigate the reality which underlies all the religions. This underlying reality is the love of humanity. For God is one and humanity is one, and the only creed of the Prophets is love and unity.

31

The Creator of all is One God.

From this same God all creation sprang into existence, and He is the one goal, towards which everything in nature yearns.

32

All are the servants of God, and all are submerged in the ocean of His oneness. Not a single soul is bereft. On the contrary, all are the recipients of the bounties of God. Every human creature has a portion of His bestowals and a share of the effulgence of His reality. God is kind to all.

33

Bahá'u'lláh has announced that the foundation of all the religions of God is one, that oneness is truth and truth is oneness which does not admit of plurality.

34

This is the unity of God; this is oneness—unity of Divinity, holy above ascent or descent, embodiment, comprehension or idealization—divine unity. The Prophets are its mirrors; its lights are revealed through Them; its virtues become resplendent in Them, but the Sun of Reality never descends from its own highest point and station. This is unity, oneness, sanctity; this is glorification whereby we praise and adore God.

35

If a soul of his own accord advances toward God he will be accepted at the Threshold of Oneness, for such a one is free of personal considerations, of greed and selfish interests, and he has taken refuge within the sheltering protection of his Lord.

36

The Fatherhood of God, His loving-kindness and beneficence are apparent to all. In His mercy He provides fully and amply for His creatures, and if any soul sins, He does not suspend His bounty. All created things are visible manifestations of His Fatherhood, mercy and heavenly bestowals. Human brotherhood is, likewise, as clear and evident as the sun, for all are servants of one God, belong to one humankind, inhabit the same globe, are sheltered beneath the overshadowing dome of heaven and submerged in the sea of divine mercy.

37

All mankind are the servants of the same God, that God is the creator of all; He is the Provider and Life-giver; all are equally beloved by Him and are His servants upon whom His mercy and compassion descend.

38

We must now realize that we are the servants of one God, that we turn to one beneficent Father, live under one divine law, seek one reality and have one desire. Thus may we live in the utmost friendship and love, and in return the favors and bounties of God shall surround us; the world of humanity will be reformed; mankind, enjoy a new life; eternal light will illumine, and heavenly moralities become manifest.

39

It behooveth thee to be content with the Will of God, and a true and loving and trusted friend to all the peoples of the earth, without any exceptions whatever. This is the quality of the sincere, the way of the saints, the emblem of those who believe in the unity of God, and the raiment of the people of Bahá.

40

All men are servants of the One God. One God reigns over all the nations of the world and has pleasure in all His children.

41

It is most certain that if human souls exercise their respective reason and intelligence upon the divine questions, the power of God will dispel every difficulty, and the eternal realities will appear as one light, one truth, one love, one God and a peace that is universal.

42

All mankind are creatures and servants of the one God. The surface of the earth is one home; humanity is one family and household. Distinctions and boundaries are artificial, human. Why should there be discord and strife among men? All must become united and coordinated in service to the world of humanity.

43

In the temple of the Lord, in the house of God, man must be submissive to God. He must enter into a covenant with his Lord in order that he shall obey the divine commands and become unified with his fellowman. He must not consider divergence of races nor difference of nationalities; he must not view variation in denomination and creed, nor should he take into account the differing degrees of thoughts; nay, rather, he should look upon all as mankind and realize that all must become united and agreed. He must recognize all as one family, one race, one native land; he must see all as the servants of one God, dwelling beneath the shelter of His mercy.

44

O ye that have minds to know! Raise up your suppliant hands to the heaven of the one God, and humble yourselves and be lowly before Him, and thank Him for this supreme endowment, and implore Him to succor us until, in this present age, godlike impulses may radiate from the conscience of mankind, and this divinely kindled fire which has been entrusted to the human heart may never die away.

45

All must be considered the servants of God; all must recognize God as the one kind Protector and Creator. In proportion to the acknowledgment of the oneness and solidarity of mankind, fellowship is possible, misunderstandings will be removed and reality become apparent. Then will the light of reality shine forth, and when reality illumines the world, the happiness of humankind will become a verity. Man must spiritually perceive that religion has been intended by God to be the means of grace, the source of life and cause of agreement.

46

All the divine Manifestations have proclaimed the oneness of God and the unity of mankind. They have taught that men should love and mutually help each other in order that they might progress.

47

God alone is Creator, and all are creatures of His might. Therefore, we must love mankind as His creatures, realizing that all are growing upon the tree of His mercy, servants of His omnipotent will and manifestations of His good pleasure.

48

All mankind are the servants of the glorious God, our Creator. He has created all. Assuredly He must have loved them equally; otherwise, He would not have created them. He protects all. Assuredly He loves His creatures; otherwise, He would not protect them. He provides for all, proving His love for all without distinction or preference. He manifests His perfect goodness and loving-kindness toward all. He does not punish us for our sins and shortcomings, and we are all immersed in the ocean of His infinite mercy.

49

We must love all; nay, we must consider everyone as related to us, for all are the servants of one God. All are under the instructions of one Educator. We must strive day and night that love and amity may increase, that this bond of unity may be strengthened, that joy and happiness may more and more prevail, that in unity and solidarity all mankind may gather beneath the shadow of God, that people may turn to God for their sustenance, finding in Him the life that is everlasting. Thus may they be confirmed in the Kingdom of God and live forever through His grace and bounty.

50

Know that the Reality of Divinity or the substance of the Essence of Oneness is pure sanctity and absolute holiness—that is to say, it is sanctified and exempt from all praise. The whole of the supreme attributes of the degrees of existence, in reference to this plane, are only imaginations. It is invisible, incomprehensible, inaccessible, a pure essence which cannot be described, for the Divine Essence surrounds all things. Verily, that which surrounds is greater than the surrounded, and the surrounded cannot contain that by which it is surrounded, nor comprehend its reality. However far mind may progress, though it may reach to the final degree of comprehension, the limit of understanding, it beholds the divine signs and attributes in the world of creation and not in the world of God. For the essence and the attributes of the Lord of Unity are in the heights of sanctity, and for the minds and understandings there is no way to approach that position.

51

As all mankind have been created by the one God, we are sheep under the care and protection of one Shepherd. Therefore, as His sheep we must associate in accord and agreement. If one single lamb becomes separated from the flock, the thoughts and efforts of all the others must be to bring it back again. Consequently, Bahá'u'lláh proclaimed that, inasmuch as God is the one heavenly Shepherd and all mankind are the sheep of His fold, the religion or guidance of God must be the means of love and fellowship in the world. If religion proves to be the source of hatred, enmity and contention, if it becomes the cause of warfare and strife and influences men to kill each other, its absence is preferable. For that which is productive of hatred amongst the people is rejected by God, and that which establishes fellowship is beloved and sanctioned by Him. Religion and divine teachings are like unto a remedy.

52

Inasmuch as our God is one God and the Creator of all mankind, He provides for and protects all. We acknowledge Him as a God of kindness, justice and mercy. Why then should we, His children and followers, war and fight, bringing sorrow and grief into the hearts of each other? God is loving and merciful. His intention in religion has ever been the bond of unity and affinity between humankind.

53

God is one, the effulgence of God is one, and humanity constitutes the servants of that one God. God is kind to all. He creates and provides for all, and all are under His care and protection. The Sun of Truth, the Word of God, shines upon all mankind; the divine cloud pours down its precious rain; the gentle zephyrs of His mercy blow, and all humanity is submerged in the ocean of His eternal justice and loving-kindness.

54

All the Manifestations of God came with the same purpose, and they have all sought to lead men into the paths of virtue. Yet we, their servants, still dispute among ourselves! Why is it thus? Why do we not love one another and live in unity?

It is because we have shut our eyes to the underlying principle of all religions, that God is one, that He is the Father of us all, that we are all immersed in the ocean of His mercy and sheltered and protected by His loving care.

55

The religion of God is one, and it is the educator of humankind, but still, it needs must be made new. When thou dost plant a tree, its height increaseth day by day. It putteth forth blossoms and leaves and luscious fruits. But after a long time, it doth grow old, yielding no fruitage any more. Then doth the Husbandman of Truth take up the seed from that same tree, and plant it in a pure soil; and lo, there standeth the first tree, even as it was before.

56

According to the teachings of Bahá'u'lláh all religious, racial, patriotic and political prejudice must be abandoned, for these are the destroyers of the real foundation of humanity. He has announced that the religion of God is one, for all revelations of it are based upon reality. Abraham summoned the people to reality; Moses proclaimed reality; Christ founded reality. Likewise, all the Prophets were the servants and promulgators of reality. Reality is one and indivisible.

57

Since the Prophets themselves, the Founders, have loved, praised and testified of each other, why should we disagree and be alienated? God is one. He is the Shepherd of all. We are His sheep and, therefore, should live together in love and unity. We should manifest the spirit of justness and goodwill toward each other.

NOTES

From the Writings of Bahá'u'lláh

1. Epistle to the Son of the Wolf, p. 43.
2. *Gleanings from the Writings of Bahá'u'lláh,* no. 84.3.
3. *Prayers and Meditations by Bahá'u'lláh,* p. 275.
4. *Gleanings from the Writings of Bahá'u'lláh,* no. 94.2.
5. *Prayers and Meditations by Bahá'u'lláh,* p. 131.
6. *Gleanings from the Writings of Bahá'u'lláh,* no. 84.4.
7. Ibid., no. 24.1.
8. *Prayers and Meditations by Bahá'u'lláh,* pp. 31–32.
9. Ibid., p. 298.
10. *Gleanings from the Writings of Bahá'u'lláh,* no. 93.13.

11. Ibid., no. 133.2.

12. Ibid., no. 160.1.

13. *Prayers and Meditations by Bahá'u'lláh,* p. 80.

14. *Gleanings from the Writings of Bahá'u'lláh,* no. 27.1.

15. Ibid., no. 162.2.

16. Ibid., no. 93.15.

17. *Prayers and Meditations by Bahá'u'lláh,* pp. 241–42.

18. Epistle to the Son of the Wolf, p. 3.

19. *Prayers and Meditations by Bahá'u'lláh,* pp. 27–28.

20. Ibid., pp. 57–58.

21. Epistle to the Son of the Wolf, pp. 1–2.

22. *Gleanings from the Writings of Bahá'u'lláh,* no. 78.2.

23. Ibid., no. 75.1.

24. Ibid., no. 45.1.

25. Epistle to the Son of the Wolf, p. 140.

26. *Prayers and Meditations by Bahá'u'lláh,* pp. 90–91.

27. Ibid., pp. 112–13.
28. Ibid., p. 316.
29. *Tablets of Bahá'u'lláh,* p. 105.
30. *Prayers and Meditations by Bahá'u'lláh,* p. 57.
31. *Gleanings from the Writings of Bahá'u'lláh,* no. 93.16.
32. The Kitáb-i-Íqán, ¶161.
33. *The Summons of the Lord of Hosts,* no. 5.43.
34. *Gleanings from the Writings of Bahá'u'lláh,* no. 29.1.
35. *Prayers and Meditations by Bahá'u'lláh,* p. 6.
36. *Gleanings from the Writings of Bahá'u'lláh,* no. 124.1.
37. Ibid., no. 113.24.
38. *Prayers and Meditations by Bahá'u'lláh,* p. 201
39. Ibid., p. 307.
40. Ibid., p. 188.
41. Ibid., pp. 111–12.
42. *Tablets of Bahá'u'lláh,* p. 96
43. *Gleanings from the Writings of Bahá'u'lláh,* no. 93.17.

44. *Prayers and Meditations by Bahá'u'lláh,* pp. 86–87.
45. *Gleanings from the Writings of Bahá'u'lláh,* no. 22.1.
46. *Tablets of Bahá'u'lláh,* p. 111.
47. *Prayers and Meditations by Bahá'u'lláh,* pp. 326–27.
48. Ibid., p. 38.
49. Ibid., p. 324.
50. *Bahá'í Prayers,* pp. 117–18.
51. *Gleanings from the Writings of Bahá'u'lláh,* no. 111.1.
52. Ibid., no. 114.15.
53. Ibid., no. 93.15.
54. *Prayers and Meditations by Bahá'u'lláh,* p. 24.
55. Ibid., p. 130.
56. Epistle to the Son of the Wolf, p. 3.
57. *Prayers and Meditations by Bahá'u'lláh,* p. 222.
58. Ibid., p. 221.

From the Writings of the Báb

1. *Selections from the Writings of the Báb,* 3:1:2.
2. Ibid., 2:31:3.
3. Ibid., 3:31:1.
4. Ibid., 4:10:3.
5. Ibid., 7:35:2.
6. Ibid., 6:1:4.
7. Ibid., 1:4:15.
8. Ibid., 7:26:1.

From the Writings of 'Abdu'l-Bahá

1. *Selections from the Writings of 'Abdu'l-Bahá,* no. 13.1.
2. Ibid., no. 36.3.
3. Ibid., no. 151.1–2.
4. *The Promulgation of Universal Peace,* p. 267.
5. Ibid., p. 43.
6. Ibid., p. 76.
7. Ibid., p. 150.

8. *The Secret of Divine Civilization*, p. 19.

9. *Selections from the Writings of 'Abdu'l-Bahá*, no. 41.3.

10. Ibid., no. 7.3.

11. *The Promulgation of Universal Peace*, pp. 208–9.

12. Ibid., p. 320.

13. Ibid., p. 216.

14. *Selections from the Writings of 'Abdu'l-Bahá*, no. 207.8.

15. Ibid., no. 7.3.

16. Ibid., no. 7.1.

17. *The Promulgation of Universal Peace*, pp. 241–42.

18. Ibid., p. 202.

19. Ibid., pp. 195–96.

20. Ibid., p. 479.

21. Ibid., pp. 234–35.

22. Ibid., p. 259.

23. Ibid., p. 89.

24. *Selections from the Writings of 'Abdu'l-Bahá*, no. 193.1.

25. Ibid., no. 2.18.
26. *The Promulgation of Universal Peace,* p. 179.
27. Ibid., pp. 552–53.
28. Ibid., p. 558.
29. Ibid., p. 414.
30. Ibid., p. 578.
31. *Paris Talks,* no. 15.1–2.
32. *The Promulgation of Universal Peace,* pp. 610–11.
33. Ibid., p. 641.
34. Ibid., p. 270.
35. *The Secret of Divine Civilization,* p. 46.
36. *The Promulgation of Universal Peace,* p. 208.
37. Ibid., pp. 660–61.
38. Ibid., pp. 90–91.
39. *Selections from the Writings of 'Abdu'l-Bahá,* no. 9.3.
40. *Paris Talks,* no. 42.2.
41. *The Promulgation of Universal Peace,* p. 109.
42. Ibid., p. 149.
43. Ibid., p. 226.

44. *The Secret of Divine Civilization*, p. 2.
45. *The Promulgation of Universal Peace*, p. 465.
46. Ibid., p. 43.
47. Ibid., p. 322.
48. Ibid., p. 447.
49. Ibid., p. 373.
50. *Some Answered Questions*, p. 146.
51. *The Promulgation of Universal Peace*, p. 415.
52. Ibid., p. 521.
53. Ibid., p. 567.
54. *Paris Talks*, no. 39.6–7.
55. *Selections from the Writings of 'Abdu'l-Bahá*, no. 23.4.
56. *The Promulgation of Universal Peace*, pp. 415–16.
57. Ibid., pp. 577–78.

BIBLIOGRAPHY

Works of Bahá'u'lláh

Epistle to the Son of the Wolf. New ed. Translated by Shoghi Effendi. 1st ps ed. Wilmette, IL: Bahá'í Publishing Trust, 1988.

Gleanings from the Writings of Bahá'u'lláh. Translated by Shoghi Effendi. Wilmette, IL: Bahá'í Publishing, 2005.

The Kitáb-i-Íqán: The Book of Certitude. Translated by Shoghi Effendi. Wilmette, IL: Bahá'í Publishing, 2003.

Prayers and Meditations. Translated by Shoghi Effendi. 1st pocket-size ed. Wilmette, IL: Bahá'í Publishing Trust, 1987.

The Summons of the Lord of Hosts: Tablets of Bahá'u'lláh. Wilmette, IL: Bahá'í Publishing, 2006.

Tablets of Bahá'u'lláh revealed after the Kitáb-i-Aqdas. Compiled by the Research Department of the Universal House of Justice. Translated by Habib Taherzadeh et al. Wilmette, IL: Bahá'í Publishing Trust, 1988.

Works of the Báb

Selections from the Writings of the Báb. Compiled by the Research Department of the Universal House of Justice. Translated by Habib Taherzadeh et al. Wilmette, IL: Bahá'í Publishing Trust, 2006.

Works of 'Abdu'l-Bahá

Paris Talks: Addresses Given By 'Abdu'l-Bahá in Paris in 1911. Wilmette, IL: Bahá'í Publishing, 2006.

Promulgation of Universal Peace: Talks Delivered by 'Abdu'l-Bahá during His Visit to the United States and Canada in 1912. Compiled by Howard MacNutt. Wilmette, IL: Bahá'í Publishing Trust, 2007.

The Secret of Divine Civilization. 1st pocket-size ed. Translated by Marzieh Gail and Ali-Kuli Khan. Wilmette, IL: Bahá'í Publishing, 2007.

Selections from the Writings of 'Abdu'l-Bahá. Compiled by the Research Department of the Universal House of Justice. Translated by a Committee at the Bahá'í World Center and Marzieh Gail. 1st pocket-size ed. Wilmette, IL: Bahá'í Publishing, 2010.

Some Answered Questions. Compiled and translated by Laura Clifford Barney. 1st pocket-size ed. Wilmette, IL: Bahá'í Publishing Trust, 1984.

Bahá'í Compilations

Bahá'í Prayers: A Selection of Prayers Revealed by Bahá'u'lláh, the Báb, and 'Abdu'l-Bahá. Wilmette, IL: Bahá'í Publishing Trust, 2008.

Baháʾí PUBLISHING

Baháʾí Publishing and the Baháʾí Faith

Baháʾí Publishing produces books based on the teachings of the Baháʾí Faith. Founded over 160 years ago, the Baháʾí Faith has spread to some 235 nations and territories and is now accepted by more than five million people. The word "Baháʾí" means "follower of Baháʾuʾlláh." Baháʾuʾlláh, the founder of the Baháʾí Faith, asserted that He is the Messenger of God for all of humanity in this day. The cornerstone of His teachings is the establishment of the spiritual unity of humankind, which will be achieved by personal transformation and the application of clearly identified spiritual principles. Baháʾís also believe that there is but one religion and that all the Messengers of God—among them Abraham, Zoroaster, Moses, Krishna, Buddha, Jesus, and Muḥammad—have progressively revealed its nature. Together, the world's great religions are expressions of a single, unfolding divine plan. Human beings, not God's Messengers, are the source of religious divisions, prejudices, and hatreds.

The Bahá'í Faith is not a sect or denomination of another religion, nor is it a cult or a social movement. Rather, it is a globally recognized independent world religion founded on new books of scripture revealed by Bahá'u'lláh.

Bahá'í Publishing is an imprint of the National Spiritual Assembly of the Bahá'ís of the United States.

For more information about the Bahá'í Faith,
or to contact Bahá'ís near you,
visit http://www.bahai.us/
or call
1-800-22-unite

AMERICA'S SACRED CALLING
BUILDING A NEW SPIRITUAL REALITY
John Fitzgerald Medina
$14.00 U.S. / $16.00 CAN
Trade Paper
ISBN 978-1-931847-79-7

A call to action for America to embrace a new society that honors the spiritual reality of the human soul.

America's Sacred Calling describes a blueprint for creating a new society that uplifts and honors the spiritual reality of the human soul while fostering the conditions for humankind to transcend the existential fears, anxieties, and petty concerns of this temporal physical world. Author John Medina examines the Western-dominated worldview that pervades so much of the modern world as we know it, and perceives a rampant materialism that is detrimental to the psychological and spiritual development of humankind. At the same time, Medina explores the writings of the Bahá'í Faith and uncovers prophecies that foreshadow a glorious destiny for the United States and its peoples. Focusing on the activities of the American Bahá'í community and the mission given to its members, Medina finds a great source of hope for the future—a future in which the American nation "will lead all nations spiritually" and play a key role in the unification of the entire planet.

FOUNDERS OF FAITH
THE PARALLEL LIVES OF GOD'S MESSENGERS
Harold Rosen
$17.00 U.S. / $19.00 CAN
Trade Paper
ISBN 978-1-931847-78-0

An exploration of the lives of Moses, Zoroaster, Krishna, Buddha, Jesus Christ, Muḥammad, and Bahá'u'lláh that examines their backgrounds, missions, teachings, and legacies, and finds the patterns that link these Founders of the world's religions.

Founders of Faith explores the lives of the Founders of the world's major religions—including Judaism, Zoroastrianism, Hinduism, Buddhism, Christianity, Islam, and the Bahá'í Faith—and reveals that they are linked by sets of striking patterns. These patterns suggest that our world's religions share universal teachings and have a common divine source. Author Harold Rosen explains how the Founders of the major religions function as the teachers of humanity; how their station differs from that of seers, visionaries, and minor prophets; and how their teachings transformed not only the civilizations that embraced them, but also humanity as a whole. *Founders of Faith* provides an examination of the rise and fall of religious civilizations, an illustrative overview of six such civilizations, as well as the background and apparent shape of the emerging global civilization.

FOUNTAIN OF WISDOM
A COLLECTION OF THE WRITINGS FROM BAHÁ'U'LLÁH
Bahá'u'lláh
$14.00 U.S. / $16.00 CAN
Trade Paper
ISBN 978-1-931847-80-3

A timeless collection of writings penned by the Prophet-Founder of the Bahá'í Faith with a universal message that all humanity is one race, destined to live in peace and harmony.

Fountain of Wisdom is a collection of the writings of Bahá'u'lláh, the Prophet-Founder of the Bahá'í Faith, in which He explains some of the "precepts and principles that lie at the very core of His Faith." Revealed during the final years of His ministry, the sixteen tablets contained in this volume cover a wide range of topics and place emphasis on principles such as the oneness and wholeness of the human race, collective security, justice, trustworthiness, and moderation in all things.

PROMISES FULFILLED
CHRISTIANITY, ISLAM, AND THE BAHÁ'Í FAITH
Nabil I. Hanna
$16.00 U.S. / $18.00 CAN
Trade Paper
978-1-931847-77-3

An examination of the promises made in both the Bible and the Qur'án concerning the coming of the Promised One.

Promises Fulfilled examines the promises made in both the Bible and the Qur'án concerning the coming of the Promised One, and sheds light on the principal objections that prevent Christians and Muslims from accepting the Bahá'í Faith. The book also discusses some of the verses in the Bible and Qur'án that are the cause of tension between Christians and Muslims. Such verses may appear to differ on the topics of Christ's crucifixion, His ascension, and the meaning of Sonship. As *Promises Fulfilled* demonstrates, however, no contradiction exists between the sacred texts. In addition, this book introduces explanations from the Bahá'í writings that can bridge misunderstandings that have arisen between Muslims and Christians, and demonstrates the shared values between the two religions. Some of the topics covered include the Word of God, the Day of Resurrection and Judgment, salvation, the meaning of life and death, miracles, parables, and the meaning of the phrase "the seal of the Prophets."

To view our complete catalog,
Please visit http://books.bahai.us